The Definitive Guide

to

Price and Volume

by Joel Pozen

Table of Contents

Dedication

To the millions who have been separated from their hard-earned money by those who by manipulation take the most out of the markets.

Acknowledgment

Neither *The Definitive Guide to Price and Volume* nor the course[1] I offer would be possible without my mentor Richard Ney. He was the foremost expert on the subject matter until his death in 2004. Mr. Ney wrote 3 New York Times best sellers: *The Wall Street Gang*, *The Wall Street Jungle* and *Making it in the Market*. He also had a bi-weekly TV show on the Financial News Network (FNN) which is how I encountered him, his books, his phone hotline and his trading course. He traded for the richest man at that time, J. Paul Getty.

As a child of the 1960's I was skeptical about Wall Street. That skepticism was borne out by Mr. Ney's trading course. The premise of his course was that the markets are manipulated. That the markets are a merchandising mechanism that professional traders use to accumulate and distribute inventory at the expense of the masses. That professionals' machinations leave footprints on all price and volume charts, regardless of the time frame. To take money out of the market(s) of a trader's choice is done by simply recognizing the pattern of how professionals accumulate and distribute inventory and "piggybacking" their behavior.

---

[1] https://besttradingstrategiesrevealed.com/prosperity-trading-course/

I would also like to thank the hundreds of students who have trusted me through the Prosperity Trading course to show them how to extract money from the market(s) of their choice. Their questions and insights have given me the pleasure of serving them and made me a better trader.

Finally, thanks to Theo Madden, my Publishing Consultant, my Proofreaders, Designers, and all the folks at BakeMyBook who made this Guide possible.

About the Author

J. Pozen learned to trade in the trenches.

Over the last 33 years, J. has invested over 10,000 hours studying charts in order to perfect the skill of pattern recognition. That experience has prepared him to help amateur traders level the trading playing field and achieve results like professionals.

After many years of learning how the moneyed elite create wealth for themselves and over 1,000 private mentoring sessions teaching others to trade the way professional Wall Street traders do, he is now providing on a broad basis this same revealing approach to those who are serious about protecting and creating wealth for themselves.

J.'s dedication to the principles of pattern recognition, as developed by the Best-Selling Author and Investment Advisor Richard Ney, has been the foundation for his ability to successfully read the market. His *Best Trading Strategies Revealed* teaches the tactics and strategies of market trading that professional traders use to take advantage of amateurs.

When Elephants Walk Across Your Lawn, They Leave Footprints

Markets are and have always been a merchandising (marketing) mechanism to separate money from the many and transfer it to the few. Markets don't move. It is the inventory objectives of professionals that move them, so they can buy at wholesale and sell at retail.

Therefore, this guide is written in that context to best convey how markets work.

Trading is not complicated. People make it that way! This guide could be 100+ pages if it were what is typically made available. Instead, it purposely is being written to be as simple, concise and short as possible.

It is ironic that trading is the biggest business in the world yet the least understood. Those who control the market have a vested interest in keeping it that way. This document discloses information you won't find in any conventional publication. As a matter of fact, you'll be hard-pressed to find this information anywhere because professionals/insiders don't want you doing what they do to take money out of the markets. The knowledge contained herein will make you the confident, disciplined trader that

Wall Street would rather you not become. The 'Holy Grail' exists within you! There is no need to search for it.

The purpose of this guide is to enable you to take advantage of the professional manipulation of all markets. These principles work in all markets, in all time frames.

Why? Because this is how the market works. Learn how to trade one market, and you can trade any market!

Professionals have no interest in your financial welfare. Price and volume analysis tells you why the market is either trending up or down. As your skills develop, you will get a feel for what the market is telling you. Price and volume analysis gives you an edge by training you to act correctly: to act in accordance with your best financial interest. You should do all your thinking prior to entering a position. Trading is not difficult if you know what you are looking at and for. Price and volume tell you what to anticipate.

The key to making money in the market is PATTERN RECOGNITION. When elephants walk across your front lawn, they leave footprints. The elephants are the professionals. The lawn is a price and volume chart. It is critical for your success and financial freedom to develop the skill of pattern recognition.

- Markets don't move. Markets are moved by the inventory objectives of professionals.
- To make money in the market, a trader must follow those who take out the most.
- The pattern recognition of professional behavior is essential to your success.
- Insiders buy on down <u>bars</u> and sell on up <u>bars</u>.
- The footprints provide the patterns to be recognized.
- Contrary to popular misconception, price leads volume. Volume does not lead price.
- If you want to know what professionals' inventory objectives are, notice how they use price to influence volume.

"Once you are able to recognize the existence of a chart formation, it should be possible for you to ascertain which professional merchandising procedure is underway and what consequences are likely to follow from it. The chart formations have as their common link the provision of "points of opportunity", that is, in an accumulation structure, several opportunities for professionals and other exchange insiders to add to their investment accounts, and in a distribution structure several opportunities to distribute and sell stock short."

- **Richard Ney**

A **bull market** – uptrend – occurs when professional accumulation of inventory is complete.

A **bear market** – downtrend – occurs when the professional distribution of inventory is complete.

Bull markets end on good news. Professionals sell on good news. It's not amateur buying that causes prices to rise. It is rising prices that cause amateurs to buy.

Bear markets end on bad news. Professionals buy on bad news. It is not amateur selling that causes prices to fall. It is falling prices that cause amateurs to sell.

"Wait to conduct your purchases until you see one day of sharply declining prices in the Dow Average (of -500 to -700 points or more) followed by a sharp decline of -200 points or more during the first 2 hours of trading the following day – or during the last hour of trading. Under these circumstances, although prices may continue lower, it will have become apparent that professionals are intent on generating anxiety and fear in order to terrorize investors into selling. Under these circumstances, you should not wait in order to try to obtain the lowest possible price. The Dow Average occupies a special place in the arsenal of weapons used by the Stock Exchange against customers. Most people make the fatal error of equating the health of the Dow with the health of their individual investments. Thus, when insiders want investors – amateurs – throughout the market

to act en masse, all they need to do to accomplish this task is to move the Dow Average dramatically. Investors, assuming the worst or best for their stock, make the mistake of buying on a sharply rising Dow or selling on a sharply falling Dow."

-   **Richard Ney**

Let the market you are trading unfold and make the decisions for you. Want what the market wants. Want what the professionals want to solve their inventory objectives.

The Market Rewards Patience and Discipline

Reading the market is not so difficult. When professional money is selling, it is not good for higher prices. When professional money is buying, it is not good for lower prices.

If you are following a future, remember that the future is a derivative of the cash market – the equity lies in the cash market and not the future. However, the future will move first because insiders will know in advance if the cash market is becoming either weak or strong and will trade the future accordingly. Since futures lead cash markets, be sure to look at the futures that are aligned with the cash instrument you are trading.

Do not be influenced by advice from well-meaning friends, brokers or the news. The only truth is price. Believe only your charts. Your charts tell you what has really happened. Charts never lie. Charts cannot be manipulated. Simply ask the right questions by knowing what you are looking at and for.

These principles were relevant 150 years ago. They are relevant today, and they will be relevant 150 years from now. Price and volume work because that is how the market works. What better way to trade than to want what the market wants? Everything you need to know is on a simple price and volume chart.

While these techniques are not secret, they are well hidden and therefore exclusive – known to the very few. Once you understand the principles that make up the foundation of the market, the market is very logical. Cause and effect are at play here. This is what enables professionals to anticipate market direction. Professionals trade with foresight, not hindsight, because they recognize patterns. Professionals ask the question, if this. The answer is then. Then is the path that pattern follows. The path of least resistance based on the inventory needs of professionals. Always follow the money!

THE MOST CRUCIAL SKILL YOU CAN LEARN IN TRADING IS SPOTTING WHEN INSIDERS ARE BUYING AND SELLING FOR THEMSELVES. It is a step by step process for analyzing their transactions so you can buy when they are accumulating inventory and sell when they are distributing inventory.

Price:

It should be self-evident that professionals want to buy low (wholesale) and sell high (retail). Exercising their control over price, they are able to drop the price of the financial instruments they want to accumulate (buy).

Conversely, professionals want to short sell high (retail) and buy low (wholesale). Exercising their control over price, they are able to raise the price of the financial instruments they want to distribute (sell).

Like professionals, you must only buy on declining (falling) prices.

A down bar is a price bar that closes either below the close of the previous bar or in a downtrend closes at the close of the previous bar or lower.

Like professionals, you must only sell on rising prices.

An up bar is a price bar that closes either above the close of the previous bar or in an uptrend closes at the close of the previous bar or higher.

Buy on strong bars (strength) and sell on weak bars (weakness).

Strong Bars – Buy in an uptrend or after the market bottoms out: Professionals buy on down bars to get the lowest (wholesale) price. Down bars are strong bars. This is especially true in an uptrend.

A down bar closing in the middle or high of the bar must be considered as an indication of strength, especially if you are now into new low ground. The volume must be very high (stopping volume). By closing in the middle or high of the bar it is obvious professionals are interested in buying the market. If the volume is low – LESS THAN THE

PREVIOUS 2 BARS – this is also a sign of strength because there is no selling pressure from professional traders. The market works on both high and low volume. Professionals either are accumulating inventory or have no interest in taking prices lower.

To stop a decline, amateurs need to be persuaded to exit losing positions. This is done by professionals rapidly dropping prices. Contrary to popular misconception, it is not selling that causes prices to fall. It is falling prices that cause selling.

Contrary to popular misconception, price leads volume!

If the volume is very high add more strength if the 'news' is very bad. Professionals buy on bad news.

Weak Bars – Sell in a downtrend or after the market tops out: Professionals sell on up bars to get the highest (retail) price. Up bars are weak bars. Especially in a downtrend.

An up bar closing in the middle or low of the bar must be considered as an indication of weakness, especially if you are now into new high ground. The volume should be very high (stopping volume). By closing in the middle or low of the bar, it is obvious professionals are interested in selling the market. If the volume is low – LESS THAN THE PREVIOUS 2 BARS – this is also a sign of weakness because there is no buying interest from professional traders. The market works on both high and low volume.

Professionals either are distributing inventory or have no interest in taking prices higher.

To stop a rally, amateurs must be persuaded to enter the market at the top. This is done by professionals rapidly raising prices. Contrary to popular misconception, it is not buying that causes prices to rise. It is rising prices that cause buying.

Contrary to popular misconception, price leads volume!

If the volume is very high, add more strength if the 'news' is very good. Professionals sell on good news.

Never forget that the market is a mirror. Whatever works on the buy side works on the sell side!

You can tell the inventory objectives of professionals by how they use price to influence volume.

Volume:

Contrary to traditional teachings (popular misconception) and what you're told by the press (a shill for Wall Street and Washington), price declines on heavy volume are bullish events. Just like price rises on heavy volume are bearish events. This is what is known as stopping volume. Every market reversal starts with stopping volume. That's because of two important facts that professionals have come to understand about amateur investors:

1) Amateurs respond to changes in price differently than they do in most other life situations. That is, they tend to buy on rising prices and sell on falling prices. Just the opposite of what professionals do.

2) The sharper the price moves, the more dramatic is the selling or buying response of amateurs.

Thus, when prices are dropped or raised little by little prices are either being "sneaked" up or down by professionals. Professionals are telling you that they are trying to avoid starting important public buying or selling. What professionals are seeking to do is to maneuver prices up or down towards their buying or selling level. When professionals have moved prices up or down to that buying or selling zone (a place where professionals and amateurs have exchanged money), a sharp rise or drop in price will often climax the rise or decline. This panics investors into buying or selling just when they should be doing just the opposite. It causes amateurs to act against their own financial self-interest. Professionals either distribute inventory when amateurs are buying or accumulate inventory when amateurs are selling. This in turn gives professionals the incentive to either launch a rally or a decline.

Markets work on either high volume (stopping volume or professional interest) or on low volume (professionals are not interested in continuing the current market direction).

Markets don't move. They are moved by the inventory objectives of professionals.

Stopping Volume:

To stop a down move, demand has to overcome the supply that is causing the down move. This, by its very nature, has to be on down bars and is seen after a down move has already taken place. That is so because stopping volume is just that: high volume that stops the movement of price and often signals a price reversal. Price reversals need confirmation. Confirmation/Permission to enter a trade is given by prices retracing their initial response to very high volume. In a top reversal, you are looking for weakness on up bars. In a bottom reversal, you are looking for strength on down bars.

At the very least, expect prices to go sideways as professionals work out the buy and sell orders while either accumulating or distributing inventory. These maneuvers take several bars to resolve themselves.

High volume on a down bar closing on the highs after a down move has already taken place would indicate panic selling from those traders on the wrong side of the market while the professionals have decided to buy this financial instrument. This accounts for the high volume and the market holding at the lows.

Any testing now on low volume at this price level becomes a very strong sign of strength in the market. No Supply.

To stop an up move, supply has to overcome the demand that is causing the up move. This, by its very nature, has to be on up bars and is seen after an up move has already taken place.

High volume on an up bar closing on the lows after an up move has already taken place would indicate panic buying from those traders on the wrong side of the market while the professionals have decided to sell this financial instrument. This accounts for the high volume and the market holding at the highs.

Any testing now on low volume at this price level becomes a very strong sign of weakness in the market. No Demand!

In a downtrend, some types of stopping volume are seen over two bars. The first down bar is on very high volume closing on the lows, while the second bar is up.

If the volume on the down bar is extremely high, this could show that there is such high selling by amateurs going on that even the professionals have been unable to absorb the selling.

In an uptrend, some types of stopping volume are seen over two bars. The first up bar is on very high volume closing on the highs, while the second bar is down.

If the volume on the up bar is extremely high, this could show that there is such high buying by amateurs going on that even the professionals have been unable to absorb the buying.

Tests: Both price and volume are tested by professionals/insiders.

There are 2 types of price tests:

On up bars, an UP-TEST and on down bars, a DOWN-TEST.

Price is tested when prices either take out the high of the previous bar and then close below the close of that bar – an UP-TEST – or take out the low of the previous bar and then close above the close of the previous bar – a DOWN-TEST.

Price tests are designed to catch stops and to mislead as many traders as possible and are normally seen after there has been weakness or strength in the background. The professionals know that the market is weak so the market is bid up to catch stops, encourage traders to go long in a weak market, panic traders that are already short into covering their very good position. Or professionals know that the market is strong so the market is bid down to catch stops, encourage traders to go short in a strong market, panic traders that are already long into covering their very good position.

Rapid price movement away from a test is done by the professionals to lock traders-amateurs out of the move. They either want amateurs to sell at price bottoms or buy at price tops!

Up-Test:

Prices are moved up rapidly and then fall back to the middle or low of that price bar.

With the appearance of an up-test, pay attention to your long positions and your stops.

Up-tests take place after a sign of weakness – high volume up bars. Contrary to popular misconception, high volume bars are generally reversal signals, not continuation of price bars. If the volume is low volume and the highs are up into fresh new ground, this adds to the strength. The news should be 'good news'.

For a market to go down, you need a top to form; you need a cause for the next move down because of professional short selling after distribution of inventory. Testing is seen after a cause has been built for the next move down. Professionals are distributing inventory and therefore have an incentive to drop prices. Up-tests are either shake-outs (remove amateurs from the sell-side) or a means of getting amateurs to buy when they should sell or to test weakness that has appeared in the market. They also catch stops and overall, they are money-making maneuvers that benefit the professional accounts. Professionals want to mislead as many amateur traders as possible.

Watch the next few bars carefully as this eventually will give you the most consistent pattern – a second wave entry. Prices drop and then retrace. Look for up bars of weakness to provide confirmation. Preferable at a point of inflection… floor trader numbers, order flow levels (where professionals and amateurs exchange money) or at a moving average or a combination thereof. That equals a stronger signal!

Down-Test:

Prices are moved down rapidly and then move back up to the middle of high of that price bar. With the appearance of a down-test, pay attention to your short positions and your stops. Down-tests take place after a sign of strength - high volume down bars. Contrary to popular misconception, high volume bars are generally reversal signals, not continuation of price bars.

For a market to go up, you need a base built; you need a cause for the next move up. Testing is seen after a cause has been built for the next move up – especially if the lows are down into fresh new ground. If the volume is low volume this adds to the strength. The news should be 'bad news'. Professionals are accumulating inventory and therefore have an incentive to rally prices. Down-tests are either shake-outs (remove amateurs from the buy-side) or to test weakness that has appeared in the market. They also catch stops and overall, they are money-making maneuvers that benefit the professional accounts. Professionals want to mislead as many amateur traders as possible.

Watch the next few bars carefully as this eventually will give you the most consistent pattern – a second wave entry. Prices rise and then retrace. Look for down bars of strength to provide confirmation. Preferable at a point of inflection… floor trader numbers, order flow levels (where professionals and amateurs exchange money) or at a moving average or a combination thereof. That equals a stronger signal!

Volume Tests:

Ignore no supply bars – volume less than the previous 2 bars – in downtrends until you see stopping volume.

Ignore no demand bars – volume less than the previous 2 bars – in uptrends until you see stopping volume.

No Supply:

A down bar with volume less than the previous 2 bars. Conversely, high volume up bar closing off its high, at or below the middle of the bar, indicates that supply is present.

There appears to be no supply (inventory/sell orders) present or demand is overcoming the supply.

This is a strong signal. To be really effective the low of this bar should be lower than the previous few bars. This creates what is known as divergence: lower prices and lower volume rather than lower prices and higher volume, which would indicate lower prices ahead unless you see stopping volume.

A fast price move down, coming back to close on the highs of the bar, especially if the low is down into fresh new ground, is a sign of strength. If the volume is low volume, this adds to the strength. The news around this time will be 'bad news'.

Do not be influenced, you have to believe your charts, not what others tell you.

A low volume down bar indicates no supply, and you would not expect lower prices with no supply after stopping volume.

Look to the following bars, what are the professionals doing.

If you're enjoying what you've read so far… then you're gonna love my mentor Richard Ney's book. A complimentary copy can be downloaded on my website:

www.besttradingstrategiesrevealed.com

You can also learn my system on creating the wealth you want by signing up for my course on the link:

https://besttradingstrategiesrevealed.com/prosperity-trading-course/

--

There is no risk to you as you are protected by our no questions asked 30-day money-back guarantee!

Top Reversal

Supply Coming In:

There has been an increase in volume on an up bar. At a new price high, at a floor trader number, at a moving average or at an order flow level prices have turned to close lower than the previous bar. These are all inflection points – where prices have a tendency to reverse course. Strong markets do not behave like this. Supply is overcoming demand.

Then you want to see an up-test (price) or a no demand (volume test) up bar during the next few bars. If so, this will confirm the weakness in the market. Waiting for and looking for these price and volume indications, a trader can anticipate the movement of prices and volume.

No Demand:

A up bar with volume less than the previous 2 bars. Conversely, a high volume down bar closing off its low, at or above the middle of the bar, indicates that demand is present.

There appears to be no demand (inventory/buy orders) present or supply is overcoming the demand.

This is a strong signal. To be really effective, the high of this bar should be higher than the previous few bars. This creates what is known as divergence: higher prices and higher volume rather than lower prices and higher volume, which would indicate lower prices ahead unless you see stopping volume.

A fast price moves up, coming back to close on the lows of the bar, especially if the high is up into fresh new ground, is a sign of weakness. If the volume is low volume, this adds to the weakness. The news around this time will be 'good news'.

Do not be influenced, you have to believe your charts, not what others tell you.

A low volume up bar indicates no demand, and you would not expect higher prices with no demand after stopping volume.

Look to the following bars, what are the professionals doing? Charts don't lie!

Bottom Reversal

Demand Coming In:

There has been an increase in volume on a down bar. At a new price low, at a floor trader number, at a moving average or at an order flow level prices have turned to close lower than the previous bar. Strong markets do not behave like this. Supply is overcoming demand.

Then you want to see a down-test (price) or a no supply (volume test) down bar during the next few bars. If so, this will confirm the strength in the market. Waiting for and looking for these price and volume indications, a trader can anticipate the movement of prices and volume.

Breakouts are often false. Professionals move prices just past previous lows or highs in prices. They do this to catch stops – amateurs place stops loss orders or enter the market just above or below the previous highs and lows and to mislead as many traders as possible – entry orders just referred to.

Trend:

The easiest and oldest means of determining trend is pivots. Not floor trader numbers which have erroneously been described as pivot points. Pivot points are actual highs and lows.

UPTREND: Higher highs and higher lows.

DOWNTREND: Lower highs and lower lows.

Study the Futures First:

We spoke earlier about how professionals knowing what will occur in the cash instruments move the futures first! Then find trading instruments that are aligned with the futures. It is a great idea to check indexes – baskets of stocks in the area you want to trade.

Quotes of Richard Ney – Neyisms:

When reading the quotes from Mr. Ney I suggest you feel what they mean. It is essential for your trading success that you make this knowledge your own – that you intuitively know it. Then market movements make sense. Then market movements will be anticipated!

How to find horses to run in the race – the trend: *"Examine the price and volume activity in other stocks in the same industry group. Pattern recognition almost always reveals an entire complex of insider planning that gives a quality of close-knit order and similarity to the chart patterns of the stocks in an industry group."*

"Do not buy stocks in which there had been an advance preliminary to an earnings announcement. If it is a good earnings announcement, Specialists will distribute stock and then sell short to supply demand at a rally high. If there are bad earnings, the stock will have been sold short prior to the announcement and then dropped. Alibis will then be employed to justify the decline in each instance. (The same is true of rumors concerning takeovers.)"

"When it is evident that there are heavy insider accumulations in a stock, accord priority to stocks with good earnings history. Specialists will ultimately use the good earnings to alibi sharp advances in the stock as it advances to its highs. The Stock Exchange has a "by-law" which demands that listed corporations inform their Specialists of any information, which might materially affect the price of an issue. Thus, Specialists are informed of news items such as earnings well in advance of their actual release. That's why good earnings announcements alibi rather than cause the sharp price movements, which precede the announcements."

This quote was included because it demonstrates how the game is rigged. Forget fundamentals and trust your charts. Professionals vote with money. Charts can't lie!

"It is necessary for all of the conditions above to be met before making your purchase of a stock (trading instrument). Then is when it is proper to enter your purchase or sell order."

Mr. Ney is referring to patience and discipline necessary to trade successfully – the skill to be able to take money out of the market consistently. Again, the market is a mirror. What works when buying the market works when selling the market. Hence the inclusion below of another Neyism.

"... the rules for buying can logically be turned into rules for selling. For instance, it's best to sell when, after a "sneaking up" period on light volume, a stock is advanced sharply to the accompaniment of major volume activity (stopping volume). Remember that these rules are simply guidelines to help discern Specialist activity and to piggyback that activity. Any technique you can develop to accomplish this task will help you, for where the Market and its Specialists are concerned, the old cliché is true: 'if you can't beat them, join them.'"

"It is no accident that most investors lose money in the stock market. Their losses are an inevitable by-product of their ignorance of how little they know about the invisible world of the Stock Exchange. Like machines dominated by external influences, they are capable only of mechanical action."

"Regrettably, the arrangements that exist to preserve the traditions and legalize the frauds of the security industry are inseparable from the general organization of a society controlled by the financial establishment, a society whose laws and principal customs have been contrived to serve the special interests of the financial community. Thus, although the Stock Exchange's most profitable practices clearly compromise the freedoms granted others by the constitution,

> *Exchange Insiders are granted immunity from the legal obligations and penalties that should be imposed on them."*

> *"Piggyback those who take the most out of the market!"*
> Richard Ney's model for stock market trading: Buy what the specialist buys, and sell what the specialist sells. As he says in The Wall Street Gang, *"I align myself with the specialist as he seeks to solve his inventory problems."*

Substitute Either Professional or Insider for Specialist

Mr. Ney used the Ticker Tape to predict future market behavior. Today computer generated charts have replaced the ticker tape, making the work easier, less expensive and faster.

According to Mr. Ney the ticker tape is essential, but:

> *"... One can understand the tape and decipher its code of communication only when experience is shaped through memory – or through the use of charts ... In the final analysis, we need both in order to make financially rational decisions."*

What is most important – critical to YOUR trading success is pattern recognition.

> *"As he moves from one phase or price level to another, however, his inventory objectives begin to reveal themselves in terms of specific trends."*

Market Trends

The specialist's objectives can be classified in terms of three trends:

a. Long-term Trend: This trend lasts on the order of years. Long-term trends have their origins in the specialist's desire to accumulate and distribute stock profitably over the years for accounts of his direct interest.

b. Intermediate-term Trend: Operating within the long-term trend, this merchandising mechanism can last from weeks to several months or more. Short and intermediate-term trends are created to solve inventory problems in the course of moving prices in the direction of a major trend.

c. Short-term Trend: This can last from a couple of days to a couple of months or more, and it can contain even shorter-term trends that can be up to several hours long. Short-term trends are a way of solving day-to-day inventory problems, while keeping longer objectives in view.

Trading Rules: 6 Things Mr. Ney Looks For To Make Trading Decisions:

1. A gradual advance in the Dow average to the accompaniment of low or medium volume, followed by a sharp increase in the Dow and overall volume. This indicates the market has become vulnerable to insider short selling.

2. A sharp advance in a stock of one or more points on a large increase in volume. Indication: the stock may be highly vulnerable due to insider short selling. Context of when written. 1 or 2 points of price movement today of a financial instrument being considered for trading may be 4 to 6 points or more.

3. A decline in the Dow average on light volume, followed by an important increase in overall volume with a sharp decline in the Dow. Indication: Insiders are accumulating stock for investment and/or trading accounts.

4. Big blocks [relative to normal volume] at or near a stock's high. Indication: Specialist short-selling is underway. Distribution! Big blocks [relative to normal volume] at or near a stock's low. Indication: Professional buying is underway. Accumulation!

35

(When Mr. Ney wrote this, a big block was 10,000 shares or more. Then as now, it is volume high enough to be stopping volume.)

5. Volume of Dow Jones Industrial Average stocks on upside and downside in excess of [a variable number shares, relative to normal]. Indication: possibility of a reversal of trend over the near term.

6. An important increase in volume as a stock penetrates an important downside price level (or pushes through on the upside). Indication: Over the short term, a rally (or decline) will occur so the specialists can dispose of (or re-accumulate) inventory. Rally (decline) can be short or intermediate terms.

Chart Patterns

According to Mr. Ney, a trader using charts can obtain from the past behavior patterns of a specialist/professional. This is an indication of his behavior pattern in the future, enabling a trader to predict what a stock or other financial instrument will do.

> *"[The] forces that determine specialist/professional activity in the past are so demanding and definable to him that they are able to exercise a dominating influence over the major direction of his stock's price in the future. Within the limitations imposed by the secrecy in which government has shrouded specialist activity, I can only speculate that these forces are related to such different elements as the trading activity in the stock, its price structure, and [its] public supply and demand. Together, these are some of the factors that give each stock its distinctive pattern as the specialist contends with them in solving the inventory problems that lie on the path of his predetermined long term price objectives."*

> *"Studying the transactions in each stock, I became immediately conscious that, on too many occasions to be a coincidence, a stock would advance from its morning low*

and then, often during the afternoon, would show an up-tick of a half-point or more on a large block of shares. This transaction seemed to herald a transformation in what was taking place, for immediately thereafter the stock would begin to drop like Newton's apple."

"At the end of several days of investigation, I discovered that these transactions at the top and bottom of a stock's price pattern were for the specialist's own account."

"The cultural response of most investors is based on the assumption that "if somebody is buying, somebody is selling"; not for a moment is it recognized that, in most cases, "if somebody is buying," it's the specialist who is selling; and "if somebody is selling," it's the specialist who is buying. Add to this the fact that investors assume that what happens to the economy or to the corporation in terms of earnings or sales determines the trend of stock prices, and you have the basis for a fallacious theory in which events in the market exist independent of each other." Because of his book, the specialist sees shifts in trends long before anyone else. This gives him a great advantage. The specialist will buy heavily at the bottom of a slide (at wholesale) then advance prices and sell, at heavy volume, at the peak of the rally (retail). He will then sell short and take prices down.

> *The turning points of a rally will be marked by heavy volume in the Dow 30.*

> *"The private investor or mutual fund can only sell short on an up-tick. The up-tick rules serves only to trap the public into selling short at the bottom, as the specialist drives the price down without a single up-tick for thepublic's use. But the specialist need not even create an up-tick to sell short. The SEC has been careful not to publicize its rule 10a-1(d), in which sub-paragraphs (1) through (9) exempt the specialist from the up-tick rule."*

> *"Who sits on the Federal Reserve Board? ... Chief officers of banks and corporations, all of whose companies are controlled by the Exchange."*

When Richard Ney's first book, The Wall Street Jungle, came out, it was on the New York Times bestseller list for 11 months. Yet the New York Times would not review it. The Wall Street Journal refused to take an ad from a New York bookstore that featured The Wall Street Jungle. All three of the major networks were wary of having Ney appear. NBC banned only two people from appearing on The Tonight Show with Johnny Carson: Ralph Nader and Richard Ney.

Not only do large banks, brokerage firms, and corporations advertise on television, they also are the largest stockholders. At the bottom of a slide, the specialist will buy heavily for his trading. After accumulation of inventory for a specialist's investment and omnibus accounts, *"His goal then becomes to raise the price of his stock with his wholesale inventory intact. In practice, though, he may have to sell shares to meet public demand. This will cause him, then, to lower the price to re-accumulate his inventory before he can proceed to higher levels."*

A rally begins while the price of the average stock is still falling. "Major rallies begin and end with the unexpected." To stimulate public demand for his stock, near the high the specialist will raise the angle of the rising prices dramatically for the stock."

True to one of Ney's axioms that prices beget volume, the public will rush into the marketplace at the rally high. The specialist can now sell his accumulated inventory to fill the increased demand brought about by rising prices. When he no longer has inventory, the only way he can meet the demand created is by short selling. Now he has the incentive to lower prices in order to cover his shorts at a profit.

"Heavy Dow 30 volume at the high is evidence of heavy short sales by the specialists. When the specialist has sold

all his inventory, and has sold short, he will then begin a downward slide of prices so necessary to his plans. Slides are a mirror of rallies. Near the bottom, the specialist will increase the angle of price decline, alarming investors, scaring them into selling their shares to the specialist who needs them to cover his short sales, and to build a new inventory at wholesale. The media will remain bullish, or cautiously optimistic throughout a slide, until the last two weeks, when they will turn suddenly bearish."

"Specialists may use a rally as a 'stalking horse' for a later rally. Price is used like a geiger counter to locate volume."

Remember, contrary to popular misconception, price leads volume!

Mr. Ney was convinced that detecting specialist short selling was a key. Specialist short selling at the peak of a rally should be detectable through increased volume.

Richard Ney used charts extensively. Ney was quick to point out that what is really being measured in his charts is not the behavior of the masses in the marketplace, but the techniques of the specialist in an individual stock as he maneuvers to solve short-term, intermediate-term, and long-term inventory problems.

> *"Investors assume that what happens in the economy or to the corporation in terms of earnings or sales determines the trend of stock prices. The most misleading element in this type of analysis is that it ignores the basic needs and motivations of the specialist system."*

To think that the market doesn't ebb and flow based on actual financial factors but is moved about so professional traders can buy and sell their inventory at your expense. Insiders rake in billions every day at the expense of the many!

You can do this too...

You can create the wealth you want so you can have the lifestyle and security you deserve!

If you haven't yet grabbed Ney's free guide, get it on my website below:

www.besttradingstrategiesrevealed.com

Since you've come this far and reached the end, you've probably liked what you've read. You may also be interested in checking out the Prosperity Trading course I am offering on the given link:

https://besttradingstrategiesrevealed.com/prosperity-trading-course/